Collected Body

VALZHYNA MORT
Collected Body

COPPER CANYON PRESS

PORT TOWNSEND, WASHINGTON

Printed in the United States of America

Cover art: Peter Paul Rubens, *Leda and the Swan,* Harvard Art Museums/
Fogg Art Museum, Private collection. 5.9.2001. Photo: Katya Kallsen
© President and Fellows of Harvard College

Copper Canyon Press is in residence at Fort Worden State Park in Port Townsend,
Washington, under the auspices of Centrum. Centrum is a gathering place for artists
and creative thinkers from around the world, students of all ages and backgrounds,
and audiences seeking extraordinary cultural enrichment.

LIBRARY OF CONGRESS CATALOGING-IN-PUBLICATION DATA
Mort, Valzhyna, 1981–
Collected body / Valzhyna Mort.
    p. cm.
ISBN 978-1-55659-372-7 (pbk.)
I. Title.

PS3613.O778625C65 2011
811'.6—dc22

                                        2011020706

98765432 FIRST PRINTING

COPPER CANYON PRESS
Post Office Box 271
Port Townsend, Washington 98368
www.coppercanyonpress.org

for my sister and Ishion

CONTENTS

Collected Body

Preface

On a bare tree — a red beast,
so still, it has become the tree.

Now it's the tree that prowls over the beast,
a cautious beast itself.

A stone thrown at its breast
is so fast — the stone has become the beast.

Now it's the beast that throws itself like a stone,
blood like a dog-rose tree on a windy day,

and the moon is trying on your face
for the annual masquerade of the dead.

Death decides to wait to hear more.
So death mews: first

your story, then — mine.

Mocking Bird Hotel

A woman's hallelujah! washes the foot of Mocking Bird
Hill, her face eclipsed by her black mouth,
her eyes rolled up like workman's sleeves.
Stirred up, a fly speaks in the tongue of the hotel
doorbell, where, on the sun-ridden straw terrace
my salvation means less than praise
to a dumb child. Damned, blinded by ice cubes,
the fly surrenders its life to the waiter's clean hands.

Behind the kitchen of the Mocking Bird Hotel
a rooster repeats hallelujah! until it loses its head.
A man harvests the Family Tree before his forefathers'
features have a chance to ripen on their faces. Parakeets
watch him from the bare nerves of the garden. He harvests
before the worms that eat his father turn into demons.

Do not eat the fruit from your Family Tree. You have
eyes not to see them, hands not to pick them, teeth
not to bite them, tongue not to taste them even in speech.
The waiter slashes the table with our bill. We descend
Mocking Bird Hill without raising dust. Dogs,
their fur hanging like wet feathers off their backs,
piss yellow smoke without lifting a leg. Gulls
smash their heads between their wings.
Light lays eggs of shadows under the shrubs.
Produce shacks stand empty like football gates.
What appeared blue from afar, turns green.
　　　　I hold it all in, even my own urine.

But the mother of vowels slumps from my throat
like the queen of a havocked beehive.

Higher than hallelujah! rising like smoke over the hill,
I scream at the top of that green lung,
        why, in the Mocking Bird
Hell, do you value your blood over your sweat,
that bitterness over this salt, that wound over this
crystal? But often to shed light on the darkness,
light isn't enough. Often what I need is an even darker
darkness. Like in those hours before the sun incriminates this
hotel, his two nostrils that illuminate our benighted bodies.

Sylt I

Lie still, he says.

Like a dog on the beach
he starts digging
until the hole fills up with water.
He has already dug out two thighs of sand
when she finally asks, what's there,
convinced there's nothing.

There's nowhere he can kiss her where she hasn't already been kissed
      by the sun.

Every evening she goes to the ocean with her three sisters and their
      old father.
They strip in a row,
                their bodies identical as in a paper garland.
Bodies that make you think of women constantly chopping vegetables
      – it is like living by the train station,
                        their father swears –
and always putting the last slice into their mouths.
For her, there is not even a knife left in the whole house.
The sound of a cuckoo limps across the dunes.
She takes a beam of sunlight sharpened side by side with stones
and cuts with it
and you can tell her vegetables from the others'
by how they burn.
Long after dinner they converse in the garden.

From above, ripened in their warm breath, plums fall about the table.
They draw the plums, one by one, like dominoes from the stock,
and sweet bones and crushed June bugs stick to the table.

By now they already stand wrapped in cocoons of white towels,
her teeth, crossed out by a blue line of lips, chatter,
scratching the grains of salt. Her bitten tongue
bleeds out into the mouth a red oyster,
which she gulps, breathless.

Their father turns away to dry his cock,
but the girls rub their breasts and crotches openly,
their hands skilled at wiping tables,
their heads as big as the shadow of the early moon,
their nipples as big as the shadows of their heads,
and black so that their milk might look even whiter.

She, too, is rough and indifferent toward her full breasts,
as if she were brushing a cat off the chair
for her old father to sit down.
They drink beer in the northern light that illuminates nothing but itself.
Sailboats slip off their white sarafans,
baring their scrawny necks and shoulders,
and line up holding on to the pier as if it were a dance bar.

It bothers her, what did he find there after all?
So she touches herself under the towel.
It is easy to find where he has been digging –
the dug-up spot is still soft.

The water is flat like fur licked down by a clean animal.

A bird, big even from afar,

believes the ocean is its egg.

So the bird sits on the ocean patiently

and feels it kick slightly now and then.

Sylt II

The wind that makes your hair grow faster
opens a child's mouth full of strawberry and sand.
Slow and sure
on the scales of the ocean
the child's head outweighs the sun.

Inside the wind –

                    a blister of a church,
its walls thicker than the room from wall to wall
where the wind shifts shade and light
as if they were two rival chess pieces
or two unmatched pieces of furniture.

Inside the church – such a stillness;
a feather which floats clenched in a fist of dust
becomes a rock by the time it hits the ground.

Organ pipes glint like a cold radiator
caged in a case carved as a tree, its branches
tied up with a snake.
Organ pedals, golden and plump, are the tree's only fruit.

It is all about the release of weight.
The player crushes the pedals like grapes underneath his feet.
My body, like an inaccurate cashier, adds your weight to itself.
Your name, called into the wind,
slows the wind down.

When a body is ripe, it falls and rots from the softest spot.

Only when a child slips and drops off a tree,
the tree suddenly learns that it is barren.

Match

are they jerking off or shaking dice
shuffling the velvet face

            of the Chess King

      back and forth
on the narrow bed — two of us
opportunely underfed

so much time killed playing bones
that our hands

          smack of meat
       so for lunch we kiss our palms
       and for dinner

          we lick

we brew tea from bread crumbs
we read time

        on domino tiles:
      from double-zero to six-six

         out of my wooden leg
      we carve ourselves a pinocchio

            of a girl
an unbendable Chess Queen

        of a girl
once swallowed

       in the heat of the game

Love

The most human sound a body can hear —
teeth being cleaned late at night across the hallway.
Even the locusts listen confused.
She too, on a bare mattress thrown over the floor,
is surprised how much of his body is in that sound —
as if she had just now noticed that he had arms.

The spit shooting down the sink —
she still counts as his body.
The noose of his saliva over her pussy —
she still counts as his body.

A suitcase of the body slapped
with stickers of scars from every location.
He folds her inside
and he ships her, and ships her, and ships
across canteens behind gas stations, across seas,
across the hands of men in blue uniform,
he ships her faster to catch the early delivery truck.

When he sits underneath her skirt
she is compelled to make confession.

Through the wall their neighbor reads the names of medications,
and she thinks the neighbor is counting precious stones:
amiodarone, zofenopril, metoprolol, mexifin.
Oh yes, she will inherit those jewels.
She will wear those jewels over her mouth to hide its twist.

But for now

he cleans his teeth and the locusts fall silent.

She lies across the hallway smelling

his long-day clothes tossed on the bathroom floor,

as his sweat crawls out of the cotton folds,

and disperses, and multiplies

like cockroaches.

Crossword

A woman moves through dog-rose and juniper bushes,
her pussy clean and folded between her legs,
breasts like the tips of her festive shoes
shine silently in her heavy armoire.

One blackbird, one cow, one horse.
The sea beats against the wall of the waterless.
She walks to a phone booth that waits
a fair distance from all three villages.

It's a game she could have heard on the radio:
a question, a number, an answer, a prize.
Her pussy reaches up and turns on the light in her womb.

From the rain, she says into the receiver,
*we stacked white tables and chairs under a shed
into a crossword puzzle,
and sat ourselves in its grid.*

The receiver is silent. The bird flounces
like a burglar caught red-handed.
Her voice stumbles past swollen glands.
*The body to be written in the last block —
I can suck his name out of any letter.*

All three villages cover their faces with wind.

Aunt Anna

I

To see Aunt Anna you have to step back; you have to
glimpse a ghost slipping through the long narrow corridor of her
body – her face vanishes as abruptly as it appears. "Today, as hours
flew by, I sat looking at Aunt Anna and suddenly recognized her,"
would be the right answer to whether you have seen Aunt Anna.
Her speech has also abstracted itself to interjections: oh – ah – no.
Even to the happiest of news, she shakes her head and weeps. Her
lips, pursed into a crescent, grow in perfect accordance with the
lunar calendar into a full moon, a white moon of an open mouth
filled with oversized false teeth. In the darkness of her face, the
moon-mouth shines, heavy with breath, that suddenly seems too
complicated a mechanism to operate. Aunt Anna, convinced that
there has to be an old-fashioned way of breathing, a manual way of
breathing, an easy way, tried and true, without the extravagances
of holding breath, or breathing hard, turns her body inside out in
attempts to bring that old breathing mechanism back. Aunt Anna
rediscovers the technique of breathing through a prayer, when her
breath sneaks in unnoticed, disguised among Catholic rhythms, and
so she patters them, one after another, believing a pause would cost
her a life.

As a young girl, Aunt Anna married into the village of M.,
three miles from P., where later my family bought a summerhouse.
The land there was so plain that playing dominoes on our veranda
I could always keep focused on M. without failing at the playing

15

board. In the early mornings I stayed out in the pasture catching tadpoles and tidying up mole casts pretending they were graves. With the approach of the dark green hours I headed back to the house shuffling my feet over the gravel. Balancing milk and blood, cows followed me into the village with all the melancholy of a funeral procession. Maple and linden trees robed themselves into their warm shadows, and stars sucked the moist belly of the sky. The lock on our metal gate thundered between my fingers announcing my return to the whole village. If the front door was already locked, I was going to get a whipping. If it was open, the night was only beginning.

Our veranda of purple jam on the reheated-for-supper pancakes; a veranda of the subtle yellow crack marking the damned double-six tile; a veranda of a thin-legged mosquito balancing on a drop of blood like Picasso's acrobat. In the distance, highway lights, softened by fog and nightfall, beaded themselves on the string of the horizon. The sunset tried to take the village into its red parentheses. And there, on the west, seemingly almost at arm's length, the flock of M.'s gardens shrunken by perspective into a single bush, as if it were the pubes of a woman, lying flat on her back, naked.

Among all of its gardens, the most beautiful garden in M. was undoubtedly M.'s cemetery. Its fence had fallen down in several places under the pulsation of sickly sweet rose shrubs and swelling buds of peonies that, extending and retracting in tune with chameleons' dewlaps, had overgrown even the freshest graves. The roses and peonies shed their seeds across the fence, often getting all the way to the village road, from where girls, playing at their future weddings, took the flowers into their backyards and onto dinner tables, spreading the oversized cemetery bloom all over the village. Girls ripped the saccharine mastic that held a bud together, and, while the premature petals unfolded, they put the mastic into their mouths and tried chewing on it when they thought no one was watching.

Every summer, in exchange for a bottle of sweet currant wine, you got us a horse carriage and took me to M. to visit your mother's grave. Your mother Yusefa, Aunt Anna's sister-in-law, was, the other way around, born in M. and married into P. several years before Aunt Anna married Yusefa's brother Adolf.

Yusefa's feet would launch thousands of miles of walking in our family. In her short life she walked from P. to M. to visit her own mother so many times, that the only thing left for her daughter was to become a limping invalid. Clouds of bumblebees thundered over the bellflowers, nipples of corn were getting harder and darker, while Yusefa walked barefoot, carrying her body, which had already erupted with five children, on the peapods of her toes, through the smell of dead-water blanketed with vegetation stronger than ice, all the way across a marshland coated with last year's hoarfrost. Eventually she became unwell, and later came down with tuberculosis, the same year the water took root in her husband's body. Drafted into a short territorial war, he was crossing the Nioman River when his horse must have stumbled, jerking itself up, a hungry pitiful horse, in that upward movement followed by a horselaugh it became a mere squalling rooster, hushed by the aggressive clapping of water. The musculature of the river held my great-grandfather forever down. His wife, coughing out our family's blood into a pillow, sent their children to an orphanage. She died and was buried in M. just before World War II.

In the cemetery, birds and flowers merged into one species. Birds sang as if a pistil were growing out of their beaks, its pollen tickling their throats; and flowers opened their mouths, dying to produce a sound. They stretched and strained their long necks, able to force out only a smell that, even though they couldn't speak, made you lose your speech for a moment.

What I remember most about those cemetery visits is how brightly lit these summers in M. were. I hold on to the conviction that it is not the light of my memory, but the sun beating so hard that it is impossible to raise my eyes to check how tall the trees are in M. The unseeable in M. starts below the tree level. This proximity gives the small cemetery the air of a convenient advantage. Once you get through the gate stalled in the hard bindweed, the unseeable is just one step up, one simultaneous eight-arms lift up in a wooden coffin. The bees suck the breath out of flowers pulling them taller and looser, wearing them out, until, swept by a single passing shadow, they fall apart. My dead keep quiet as if they had been buried facedown, and decompose with grace and decency.

After the cemetery you took me to a blue house, its door
thrust wide open by a woman – her breasts like the Ural Mountains
separating her face from her body. She moved with brisk loudness,
dressed in so many layers flaring one under another, sweaters
and shirts opening like doors into new rooms and floors, that
it seemed the blue house itself lived inside her, not the other
way around. She invited us in – the mudroom revealed rows of
milk cans filled up to the brim and covered with carefully cut
squares of yellowish gauze. The smell of motherhood around that
woman – the mudroom was its source. Daily milking with her
forehead pressed against the cow's side like a child hunched over a
piano. Milking the white piano keys into a can, giving each teat a
drowning man's grip. The steam rising over the milk warmed by
the cow's blood – the same steam that rises over its manure, like a
halo which crowns indiscriminately the saint and the disturbed. To
which does motherhood in M. belong? Sanctity or disturbance; milk
or manure? Mothering a child into a country unfit for history, as
if history were the kind of fruit which required a warmer climate,
a richer soil, abler cultivation. A child who, before learning her
own name, would learn that history had to be tangible like meat
at dinner, but like meat at dinner, it also remained an abstraction,
a dinosaur; meat and history, two sins of luxury against the local
absence of religion.

Mothering a child into the land one cannot walk to, nor fly
to, nor swim; the land reachable only through a mother's womb,
which is a dangerous road and many die trying. Mothering a child
into the land where the grains of sand are still being separated
into those that would become stones and those that would grow
into mountains; where birds are so huge, their crests are a herd

of galloping horses, and their eyes take a day to close and another day to open; where grass is so tall, it is deemed as the underworld; and, underneath the grass – the lightning of roots, the cable where electricity lives like a mammal that knows its way into the quietest house, where it steals the dark and eats the cold. You were mothered into this, in the kitchen, where bread was being baked, and the mothering Yusefa, steaming with blood and sweat, raced against the kindled baking oven. The moment your head showed, a sudden spasm of smoke from the oven erased the room, and your blinded mother couldn't decide what to deliver first: a loaf of bread or a baby. Somebody must have thought there still was a chance to erase that moment from the face of the earth, to start blank, to redraft, to replace a kitchen with a hospital in Paris and call you Serge Gainsbourg, or in Chicago – James Dewey Watson; you could have been the king of Malaysia, or several weeks old in Italy, you could have become a casualty of a bomb attack against Mussolini, you could have been swept by three earthquakes, but your grandmother whiffed "a girl!" and that word began your world of low log houses ingrained in the black soil, where you learned the meaning of pink from a cow's nipple, the meaning of maroon from a boiled beet, and the meaning of blue from a dead man's body. Born in a caul, you were promised wealth, health, fool's luck, and bird's milk. In truth, you had dragged the caul with you because you knew what misery and need awaited outside. The caul was your only chance at having something of your own. You smuggled it out of a womb. You were born already a suitcase-trader. On your exit from the vagina, you were caught, undressed, and rinsed with a stream of smoke.

Your mother keened with her squirrel hands at her face. Or maybe I'm retelling it wrong. Maybe those were not the squirrel hands that she had, but two front squirrel teeth: the tooth of good and the tooth of evil. She bit them through you, threaded a needle through the bites, and sewed you to that soil like a button. And so that you didn't have any doubts, she threw over your head – a noose.

First thing, the woman seats us in the kitchen of the blue
house. Clusters of grapes stare into the windows like blistered
lepers. The smell of bittersweet geranium from the windowsills
saturates all the food. Most – sausage, eggs, fresh bacon, smoked
chicken – come out wrapped in newspaper pages dated five to ten
years ago. A wind-lashed farmer extending cupped hands full of the
year's first harvest as if he were about to wash his face with it; a
driver trying out a new thresher; a midwife pressing two loaves of
newborn twins to her breasts. Faces of missing persons, deformed
faces of unidentified victims, even among the dead there's rarely a
mouth without a smile, even rarer – a mouth with regular teeth.
All these people are mummified according to the unique method
of stuffing their paper-thin skin with homemade meats, eggs, and
the pinkies of pickled cucumbers, immortalizing their twenty-
four hours of daily-paper glory with the flesh of animals fed with
the crops these people have harvested with their bare hands and
their new shining machines. Stains of grease show through the
yellowed paper as if the stuffed bodies were already breathing on
the hoarfrost of print. The woman skins them again, cuts them
up, their meat still thinking in provincial journalistic clichés as it
approaches our three willing-to-listen mouths.

You have to always sit at the very corner of the kitchen
table, its arrow pointing onto your belly – your belly, on which
nobody would ever place high stakes, wins every time. You sit
fidgeting that corner – your idea of showing respect to the house;
on the edge of the chair, your right leg unbendable. If you had an
arm that didn't bend at the elbow, it would have made it easy to
simply choose begging, but it was your leg that was always thrust
ahead of you like the stick ahead of the blind. You tricked it only

once, when, on the way to the surgery, you asked the driver to stop the ambulance car at the registry office, borrowed the whites from the nurse, and got married. Pashka had fallen in love while reading your letters over your brother's shoulder in the aviation college somewhere in Russia, and arrived a day before the surgery, with three kopeks and a toothbrush. "What an ugly man, what a beautiful girl," the doctor said when he opened your knee like an oyster.

The surgery was initially scheduled for the first week of July – the July you were fourteen. In March, the dying Yusefa sent two of your brothers, and you, to an orphanage. The youngest had to be placed in a separate institution for children under five. The oldest, Vaclav, had been staying with relatives in Poland since Anton's death. He was later evacuated to Mordovia, from where, once the war was over, he walked by himself to Moscow to enroll at the aviation college.

On June 21 you dreamed of entering a crowded house, Yusefa walking toward you across the room with two buckets filled with water to the brim, and woke up torn with the pain of seeing your mother alive, the fear that she wanted to soak you, and the two-full-bucket promise of good fortune. The night of June 22, hurling back sleep, you got out of bed, dressed, woke up your brothers Yanak and Kazik, marched with them straight into the headmistress's bedroom, and announced that you wanted to leave for P., to stay with Aunt Anna's sister Viktsya. The headmistress, through sleep, moved her head just slightly, but nevertheless enough to be read as permission. Hastily, without looking at each other, the three of you took off your shoulders the long sleeves of the orphanage corridors, the pleated skirts of its silent staircases, the worn-out collars of its windowsills – left all of this to the sleep of the children whose chests moved up and down in breathing meant not for living but only to fan away hunger. Death, like a spoiled child to whom nobody ever said "no," was already licking the cream off their sleeping lives, leaving behind the bland crust of their bodies.

You took the first bus, reaching the village two hours later. Chasing the bus, pages of paper flew framed into fire; books, newspapers, photographs, postcards flew all the way to P. from that city where the wind was on fire, where the red pencil of fire was filling in the centuries-old crossword of window grids. The unanswerable was answered by fire that morning. Even where there were no questions posed, fire was the answer.

Blood rolled out of bodies like a red rug for the fire to walk on. First, the city, like a marble elephant, dropped on its knees, and then the buildings bared their hollowed heads and drained themselves into the eye sockets of the sleeping dead on the ground floors. The hungry rushed to the borders where they eagerly gorged on bullets, stuffed themselves with the bullet rice until their weight pulled them down and they could no longer get up.

Viktsya, a heartless woman; since her birth, death stood
behind her left shoulder knocking on her body – knock-knock,
knock-knock, knock-knock. She learned to trick death by what her
body could give without giving itself – her children, newborns,
handed over one after another. She cried on top of their graves
until they came into her dreams begging her not to drown them in
her tears. She took you, among other orphaned relatives, and for
four straight years fed you boiled water.

In four years you could not make a step by yourself. The
rot showed from underneath the bluish knee like the tumid face
of your drowned father flowing slowly under the still waters. A
beautiful man, even bloated with water and the blood of horses and
soldiers: a woman washing herself in the river could have taken
his face for her own reflection and smiled to herself in peace. In
the kitchen of the blue house in M. his unframed portrait hangs
alongside a reproduction of Vasnetsov's *Alyonushka*.

All the furniture is painted white, with brown shades of
dirt along the brushstrokes. In the crack between a mirror and
its frame, a yellow bouquet of curve-edged photographs leaves
no space for reflection. Every curtain in the windows and in the
doorways, every sofa, apron and napkin, every rug and mat, every
cup, kettle, and every inch of the wallpaper is densely covered with
a flowery pattern of every shape: roses, lilies, dahlias, daisies of
every size and color, the lifeless blooming of my youth, the pattern
that offends nobody, the pattern that means nothing, the fastest
answer to the request for beauty.

While the blooming is transported inside the house, the front yard and the garden are cramped with indoor furniture: in the tall grass a big armchair stands swollen with rainwater. Rainwater also comes to the brim of a large rusty bathtub, which has no other purpose than catching falling leaves. While in the kitchen, cupboard doors and drawers open and close, making their own distinct moans, releasing teacups, plates, sugar bowls, and cutlery, the two women inventory our extended family, mentioning their aunt Anna only briefly – so evasive is Aunt Anna's body, it is impossible to hold a thought of it for longer than an instant. The plastic tablecloth has a pattern of exotic fruit. I eat sausage and stare through a many-faceted glass.

A century ago Aunt Anna got married in M. Hard to believe there was once a train going through the village. It was on the train that they put Aunt Anna with her handsome and wealthy husband Adolf – that same Adolf who, stung by a bee in one eye, would, out of natural aesthetic inclination, catch another bee to restore the symmetry of his face – and all she managed to do was to pass little Yadzenka into Kazik's hands through the compartment window. It was Yadzenka's second birth: her skinny genderless body pushed by her young mother through the window gap toward her not-that-much-older cousin – out and, this time, truly away from the womb. Whether Yadzenka gave a long newborn's scream toward the leaving train, I cannot say. Kazik brought Yadzenka to the house, his parents already in hiding; the removal committee came upon six children sitting on the cold stove-couch, asked for somebody to sign the removal papers, but none of them could write. Thus they remained in P. while Aunt Anna's train went all the way to Tyumen and beyond it, into the Siberian woods which Aunt Anna learned to gather, cut, saw, hew, drag, and pile. On the cleared land they sowed millet and, returning to the barracks after work, Aunt Anna covertly plucked the spikelet, rubbed it between her palms, and cooked it into a soup. When Adolf and their newborn died of hunger, Aunt Anna decided to run away.

Aunt Anna, who once married into M. and had walked three miles from P. to M. every weekend, walked 1,730 miles from Tyumen back to P. This time she walked there for no man, for no village girl's dreams of the neighboring village; this time she walked for the memory of that pubes, for what it concealed – the source that her mouth was so hungry to embrace. When she came into her mother's backyard, all she wanted to do was to eat.

Cast-iron barrels were filled with beets and potatoes for pigs, and Aunt Anna ate with pigs, standing before the barrels with pigs, on her knees with pigs; knees, small and sharp like two millet grains planted into the dirt and manure. She ate so much that her belly couldn't stop growing – it swelled larger and larger, until it became Aunt Anna's younger brother. Aunt Anna walked from house to house complaining about her brother's bad health. When she got stronger, somebody wised her up to take her brother and go straight to M. to claim Adolf's house. In M. both of them were arrested and taken to jail. From the jail they were taken to the train that went 1,596 miles toward the Urals.

In Nizhny Tagil, Aunt Anna worked at a Railroad Car Works, manufacturing freight cars that were to transport people and lumber across the incomprehensible country. Later she remarried and at family kitchen tables was inventoried as free and happy. She had another child, maybe even two, but as for Yadzenka – Aunt Anna never wanted her back. After the war Aunt Anna returned and moved from one house, like the blue one, to another, until she settled down and started working at a calf barn. Yanak went on foot to P. from Berlin. Instead of a usual triangular envelope with a hand-drawn airplane and inscription, "Greetings from Air," a telegram arrived from an aviation college somewhere in Russia: "At the hospital. Unwell. Alone. Please come."

Yanak, without washing the blood and foul off his feet, without picking splinters out of his heels, without waiting until skin grew back on his soles, went jumping from one freight train to another heading to Moscow, Vaclav dying alone, in pain and hunger. (In far-off lands there lived a King and his Princess

daughter for whose hand competed three Princes – the eldest
Solitude, the middle Hunger, and the youngest brother Death.)
Kazik announced that for several nights he had been waking up to
see Yusefa sit at the edge of his bed stroking his feet, and shortly
thereafter, when running across the street, was hit by a car. Yanak
died fifty years later, beaten and robbed by his own grandson.

You weeded and clipped the rosebush at M.'s cemetery,
and, though always calm and collected, you would, just for an
instant, break into a lament, short but excruciating, as if you had
choked on a flower seed or raised your eyes too high into the
unseeable:

I rest on the pillows embroidered by you, Mama,
while worms embroider your resting body,
stiff as a doll I'm still small enough to play with,
to spoon-feed the soil that has been shoveled
over your young mouth.

II

As I write this, I imagine you are here with me, at the North
Sea, on an island shaped like a ballerina, frying potatoes on both
hemispheres of a tiny stovetop. At sunset, the birds at the edge of
the water are black, but their shadows are purple. A girl jumps
cold waves holding her hands up like a candelabrum. Have you ever
noticed this about the north? The heat can fit into a tip of coal or a
tongue, into one cigarette butt, into one red button that guarantees
the eventual boiling of water, into that thromb of space allocated to
it here – this tiny sun, bruised into the lavender neck of the sky with
a brute thumb. But, as for the cold, it calls for vastness. Cold needs
absence – even speech, a phrase like "how to stop thinking about
you without stopping to think" can startle the cold. It needs dunes of
bleached vegetation falling down in rows of ivory dominoes; it needs
dog-rose bushes nailing their buds to the soil with their own thorns;
it prefers the flatbreads of fish bodies to the curves of the animals.
The cold needs a sea – this polonaise in Gray-flat minor, this gray flat
wing of an injured bird still trying to lift itself up while being pecked
relentlessly by its own kind. The sea unburdens the cold, unsaddles
it, lets it loose, the sea carries the cold as the cold gains speed, as
it stretches, as it unfolds, like a handkerchief rushed to a bleeding
child. Stripped of warmth, freed of any expectations to shed itself,
the northern light is a separate part of day and night, their third,
out-of-wedlock sibling, the yellow time that does not illuminate but
color. The sun caught into the web of the northern light is merely
an insect quivering and struggling for many hours to free itself, until
it finally gives up and steps down, and for the rest of the season it
hangs across the sea like the cut-off head of a city criminal thrust on
a stake on the opposite side of the Amstel river.

The sea is the land, only skinned. You look away, avoiding
my eyes, in such sweet misery – an opera singer catching her
breath – then slide your eyes on to your perpetually tanned hands
that are already fidgeting the edge of your shrunken pink cardigan.
As a child I dreamed you being raped in this pink sweater, lying in
a ditch behind our summerhouse, your unbendable leg thrust into
your body like a shovel, your mouth opened without a sound and
staring at me like your third eye. I didn't even know what rape was
back then. All I knew was that your pink sweater was your way of
showing others you were not a pauper.

"A poem named after Aunt Anna, pages about Aunt Anna,
and not one word about Boleska" – the clock on the wall sounds
like a leaking faucet, drop after drop measured with striking
precision. The journey made by your voice is as long as the journey
of light. (Boleska, if you are reading this, please find me, everybody
is dead.)

"When I'm back, let's go to M. together."
"To M.? What did you forget in M.?"
"Yusefa's grave might need tidying up."
"To go across the country to prune a rosebush?"
"It is a very small country."

The two of us here, on the parting from where the sea is
combed in one direction and the sky in another, from where the
sea casts its shadow – the wind – over the rest of the world, on
this scar on the skin of landscape, on this strip of skin showing
from under the gray garments of the planet. The waves thrown
generously, at no interval, the sea bailing the water out trying

to save itself from drowning, but then, at once, rushing to claim
its own back. The sea which, in its restlessness, only waits for
the right moment when it could get up and walk out of here for
good. Your mother who sits on the bench in front of the house
and coughs out red crumbs of blood hastily picked up by hungry
birds. Your mother rolled up on her deathbed, folded along every
joint, ready to be shipped away, ready to be a light load, ready
to return everything she has been given – this body, already less
believable than its own shadow, while its shadow can still break
the window against which it is cast. This face that explains beauty
in the simplest lines, these curls – as if somebody had emptied an
overscribbled diary over her head; she brushes its words off her
face, scratches them off her neck, spits them out of her mouth,
her face is already only a fist that death is trying to unclench, her
senses already tuned to a different frequency – she is cold when it's
hot, and hot when it's cold, sour tastes bitter, bitter tastes salty,
but nothing tastes sweet enough. Outside, the saw of the forest
line cuts in two the immaculate spring sky. Cows howl, smelling
through the cracks of the barn the wet mouth of the waking earth.

Boleska, forgive me this time.

Unter den Linden

to Vladek

She folds her arms where one day her chest will fold into breasts,
if that's something women in her family have secured,
if theirs hung, and had chapped-elbow teats.
She folds her arms because in a house
of such uneven walls nobody
should be expected to learn handwriting.

Her uncle limps, stutters, and winks. The clock's hands
fold in a prayer when he comes to eat
a dish bleached in sour cream, to place his chewed
bread over her bruised
letters. On the veranda steps
he lifts her up and breathes into her face
a German song about Russian rivers.

This land and sky are glued together with the pressed-out guts
of a butterfly dried between them —
a one-street village with wings of gardens to each side.
She holds her pen like a spoon. Her pursed lips
frown at the horizon line.

Two lindens keep the kitchen window busy.
One day, her uncle sings,
                    whole street of lindens!
You will be running from the man who lies
                    inside the ripped-open body of a bathtub,

when a whole street of linden trees

                                        steps out of night

like all the women he has ever had,

they hold out their bodies like towels,

and whisper: take us, sister, dry him with us.

That's when she'll wipe her hands of sweat and ink.

Photograph

Sochi. 1982.
They stand
hand in hand
with the confidence of an excellent grade
on a report card.

Out of the corner of their eyes
they might see the beach,
a boy hiding behind a slice of watermelon –

                                his ancient red fortress.

Preoccupied, he peers through the pit holes
waiting for his enemy to approach.

His enormous mother reads a list of passengers from the crashed
        airplane,
how their blood went up
like a boiling thermometer
and horror no longer had a signifier.
Under her sweaty palms, the print blurs,
turning into black body bags
arranged on the page.

Honeymoon.
Hand in hand
they stand in Sochi in 1982.
She thinks to herself:
my Lifeline is not on the palm of my hand,
but bent slightly in the knee,
it's my leg lifted over my man's body.

How natural it is for a Lifeline
to start where a leg does.

Between the shots, in her mind's eye
she considers the line's length,
and smiles into the camera with relief –
for her legs are long.

On the beach
the watermelon fortress
stands sweet,
undefeated,
blood invisible on its red bricks.

My Father's Breed

It's four in the morning.
I'm ten years old.
I'm beating my mother between the mirror and the shoe rack.
The front door is ajar. A bridge
presses its finger to a frozen strip of water.
Snow falls over it gritting like sand on glass.
Both of us, in our long nightgowns.

I stare into her earring hole and aim
at her large breasts not to hurt my knuckles.
I slap her face like I flip through channels.

My father lies at the door. From his shirt
lipstick smiles at me with the warmth of urine.
It's as if somebody threw at him slices
of skinned grapefruit.
Every time she hits him – I hit her.
Look at this. Look whom you've bred.

How can he see from under his pink vomit.
But his body smiles –

cannot stop smiling.

Utopia

have you seen a girl with blue hair?
have you seen my Malvina?

after sunset
our town is deserted like a train station
in its schedule there's nothing
but the sun and the moon

the ocean rushes at seagulls
like a dog on a leash
and the tower clock clears its throat every hour
but never dares to speak out

and till the next dawn
lovers fix our bodies
with saliva — they oil our pores
with hands — they repair our faces
that is why we don't look anything like each other
we are handmade

during the day the waves curl up like the locks
of blue-haired Malvina
and we brush them with our soft bodies

we welcome you to the colony of the sun
whose yellow flag — a glass of lemonade! — waves over every table
the ocean massages the planet's core
and the night waits through the day in our black hair

in the afternoon our blood boils
and pours out through our noses and mouths
onto white ocean stones
turning them into red apples
and we offer those apples to our lovers
and they break their teeth against them

this is why we know neither good nor evil
sometimes our words can cut meat

when we are betrayed
we go deep into the water
and watch how our heartbeats
scramble the ocean into foam
and throw high waves on the shore
where children drown

and again the moon hangs like a white cocoon
so that at dawn a red moth will open its wings
and come down to the brook
and our men try to subdue it
they jump on its back
like overripe plums falling from trees
to tame the horse of the planet
and then with their lips dry from thirst
they rush to our mouths
and through them
they pull out our hearts
like buckets full of cold water
out of wells
and then they let them fall down with a roar

and this is why our hearts ache

if a heart could be pulled out like a tooth
if memory could be killed
we'd have been so happy living
under the yellow lemonade flag

and the new day is at the town gates
like a trojan horse
that carries inside it the whole army of the sun
our men take it to the central square
their naked bodies like god's index finger
and our love to them is dangerous and blind
like a wasp that swarms around the house

we eat malachite grapes
and waffles thin as a spider's web
and the sun marches through the town
wearing a triangle of birds – a napoleon's hat

when it gets dark
we put ocean shells to our ears
and listen
holding our breath
to Malvina
        her head shaved bald
        who weeps while picking up in the dark
        blue locks of her famous hair

Guess Who

i found healing

when
having gone blind
you put your hand on my face
just to make sure

should i be ashamed of myself?

to return to your room for my own sake
transparency like eczema spreading all over your body
pain that always gets you like a ball in a children's game
i come without regard for what it takes you
to lift your arm and hold it like that
while i stand there and
in a voice not mine
whisper
guess who
guess who
guess who

Zhenya

Jags of marble stairs in the night drizzle. Water irons dim
squares of glass. Leaves under poplar trees eat through the soil's
crust and sink deeper into the ground. The clicking of heels,
guttural and tight, rises from somewhere underground and stops
suddenly at the body. The impassability of the body moving into
the leaving, painting the leaving with confident dark strokes. Until
the exit swallows it – gulp. On the squares, fountains are empty in
triumph. The city breathes, marble and ageless.

The reservoir, rasping its scales, detunes the synchronized
routine of the prewar trams. Gutter-birds on the curb,
indistinguishable from lumps of mud – you have to kick them slightly
with a tip of your shoe to see if they fly off or fall. A bus doesn't
come for a whole hour. When it arrives, it is a washing machine.

School started a month ago. In the morning, the picture of
a smoker's liver steps out from the seventh-grade anatomy book
and right into the sky, where it flows fast and in all directions. On
the radio, police reports describe kids who went to school and
never came back. Thin, five feet tall, with a caterpillar of a scar
where the appendix had been cut out. Face – average. In navy blue
trousers. All as one dressed in navy blue trousers. Went to school
in their blue trousers and never came back.

In a couple of weeks the opera house will open for the new
season. Its massive porous building, a worn-out white sponge,

absorbs the damp air of the dark park, its marble stairs kaleidoscope under the pools of water. The fire of raindrops sores the bullet cavities on its walls. Inside, a janitor smears the dust over the stage. From time to time the costumes are shaken up by the hurried footsteps along the carpeted corridors. Shortbread cookies are being reordered for the still deserted cafeteria.

Zhenya moves as if her left side were heavier than her right. She leans like an old village fence, almost kissing the ground, and a shred of green cloth, scudded by the wind around the grazing, has finally caught hold of one of the boards and hangs on it – Zhenya's jacket. Enveloped by the damp October soil, under unending drizzle, the fence is rotting. Leisurely, Zhenya rots at a forty-five-degree angle, her putrid insides wrapped carefully into her skin. Unable to tear my eyes off Zhenya, as she limps away, stops to thoroughly read the university announcements, smokes leaning against the corner of the International Affairs building, I imagine God's invisible hand that carries the white paper wrap around the city, unable to find a proper trash bin.

Zhenya has an illness. She conceives space inadequately. During the class she excuses herself to go to the bathroom, and later, unable to find the way back to her desk, tumbles around from one desk to another, like a note with a drawing of a naked professor. We sneak a look and giggle through our closed mouths. For us, Zhenya's body disoriented in space is a space of its own. Her face looks as if her features have taken one step forward. Lips stir in a tidal movement, always salted with bits of saliva. Before every class Zhenya refreshes her mascara, aiming it straight into her eyeball, like a gun. In the proximity of her body it is permitted not to hold anything back, permitted to call things by the names that first come to mind. In fact, no rules, no laws, no constitutions apply in the radius of Zhenya's shadow. We can be animals. We can move and talk the way we won't dare to, even with our unseasoned lovers.

Zhenya doesn't like breaks. There's nothing more terrifying than the transition from one classroom to another. God bucks up, sighs, and drags Zhenya through the long university corridors. A thousand times passes by the correct door, a thousand times turns around, calculates the trajectory of getting into the doorway, launches her body forward, and a thousand times runs her face into the wall. The world of doorframes, corridors, staircases, and roads appears before Zhenya as a reflection of the moon in the dark water. She approaches that world, but the world caught in the tremor of her labored breathing confuses Zhenya; she reaches out for it, first cautiously, as if she were checking on a sleeping animal, then – insistently, aggressively, she knocks on the air, demands the air to open itself into something to walk through, to sit on, to lean against; she beats the air in order to harden it into a knob, a desk, a hand, a shape.

Zhenya likes to talk about men. The way her eyes roll up a little too high when she utters an obscenity, and she has to shake her head in a movement of passionate agreement to bring her eyeballs back to my face level. She says, your boyfriend looks like Alain Delon. It seems that the words that come from her mouth have been lying there stored for months, or even years. They emerge as thin bubbles of odor and saliva, and she has to breathe harder to shake those bubbles off her lips until they finally pop up

— looks! like! alain! delon! He looks like his mother, I say. Do you want to marry him, she asks. Of course I do. Is he good in bed, she asks again. And I don't know if I should reply or ignore her.

We come to grammar class, already exhausted at nine in the morning. From the earliest moment of waking up, this city reflects our faces in the windows of its shops, doors, and buses; it rains and rains because the city wants to reflect us with its every surface, wants to turn all of itself into a distorting mirror, but most of all it wants to reflect us in the faces of other people, to make us recognize how we all share a certain smudge, a typo, an almost invisible defect. It is not a broken telephone, but a broken mirror. Every one of us is nothing else but a reflection of a reflection of a reflection of the first defective person: first person who stands in front of that first mirror unable to grasp where it is she is placed, unable to decide which way to move away from this site of confusion, too confused to understand who has to move first – her reflection or herself.

We take our seats and joke idly. Zhenya, in the majestic vessel of her body, tries to loosen the narrow aisles between the desks; she moves lubberly, but with great concentration, a smile leaking over her face with every slight advance. Finally she lifts up all her possessions and places them on top of the desk, and, as if from an open wound, thick pink yogurt gushes out of one of her bags. Yogurt beats against the floor, desks, chairs, blackboard, Zhenya's clothes, and we do not hide our laughter. We cackle, and the pink liquid jets into our faces, scores into our wide-open mouths.

Zhenya fusses around the classroom, flooding everything on her way. She cannot find the door to run out to the bathroom.

Zhenya, to the left!

And she turns to the right.

Oh no! Go back, go back now!

The other way! Follow me!

Here, Zhenya!

But Zhenya follows nobody. It is we who, after years of the same image gushing at us through mirrors, windows, and water, are finally pushed to reflect Zhenya in our own distorted ways. Stepping into a shower, I have often fallen into a trap of doubt – is it indeed a shower cabin or, possibly, a desk in my classroom? What if I were standing like that, naked, bloated, and sweaty, on top of my desk during grammar class, reaching for the ceiling lamp, confusing light with water, laughter with the sound of water hitting my body? I cover my breasts with my left hand, scoop a handful of my genitals into my right, and walk around the apartment peering into things for fear of recognizing my classmates in my furniture.

Looking for Zhenya I find you. Walking through a door, I walk into this kitchen where nobody bakes, where chairs are not built for sitting, a table not meant to hold a thing. I hear your face, behind the tall dam of your fingers, gathering strength and speed. I follow your heavy sigh all the way to the floor. The boards are painted a muted orange, books are marked with socks, a beam of light overturns a surprised jug.

What is love if not a need for a beholder, a witness; if not the possibility to be immortalized in the story of another person? The insect caught in a drop of amber knew what it was doing. Neither helper nor bystander. Your blood runs like a tape of an implanted recorder. You are my plan for immortality. The audience for my privacy. I'm molding you into a gravestone of all the words and images of myself I won't be able to sustain forever. You, who recite from memory every poem you ever read – I'm set with you. You will be trying the crystal shoe of those movements and words on the foot of every woman crossing his path, because this is how love works – a man looks for the same woman in many women, and a woman looks for many men in one.

I turn around to look at you. Am I good in bed, I ask. And you chuckle.

II

At the end of August we take a fat white bus to the
countryside where my distant uncle has a house that remembers
my well-fed, then starving, then well-fed, and then starving again
grandmother; and a garden planted in a different language and
century. All those years of the unmatched harvests of marbled
plums, white apples, birch syrup, and raspberries we used to wear
as thimbles. In the center of the garden a pear tree stands since
World War I, tasted by no one. Pears were tiny like baby fists,
hanging firm, green and hard; then one night – everybody sleeping
– they suddenly ripened, fell to the ground, all as one, and by the
first rooster were already rotten. The mawkish decay under the
pear tree attracted big black butterflies that sucked it, making the
rot bubble with their impatience. Nothing could scare them off. A
child, I would slip out of my sandals and walk over that marshland
under the tree, savoring the moist softness of rot and the sharp
crackle of the butterfly wings under my bare feet.

He says, take the plums, the garden stays pitch-dark even
at noon because of the plums this year. He stands like that, rough
and real, alone, without even a dog. The garden, disseminated,
overgrown, keeps on producing out of its own insanity. The
flowers bloom in colors we are shy to look at. The fruit falls on the
grass constantly, each carried by its weight, softness, and sound. In
the house, he stays in one room and keeps the rest of them locked.
He smiles like a man who hasn't smiled enough. His stutter – I
used to think he was trying to laugh through speech. He tells you,
come, city boy, and pulls out three many-faceted glasses. At the
table he stutters through what a special guest you are and all that.
We toast something – I won't remember.

Time can penetrate houses like that only on the waves of a radio or an electric heater. Both are broken: the house rests in stagnant time. The body's movements lose their meaning and just grow from the body turning into its new limbs and curves.

He shakes the trees and you and I dive underneath and collect the plums into plastic buckets. He shakes again, and a purple night falls over our heads. I try to keep my eyes open to distinguish your figure bent beneath the trees. We take the darkness apart, one plum at a time, exhaling loudly like men saved from drowning. And he shakes the trees again and again. Night and day, night and day, night and day. When we finally emerge, with our buckets full, five years have passed.

III

When I think back at what happened between us then, I
cannot get rid of Zhenya, in a stray green jacket over her spongy
body, trotting across the campus. Zhenya, breast-feeding us with
her pink yogurt, baptizing us in the waters of her saliva. Then I
think of the kolkhozy and kolkhozy of cow pastures, of coltsfeet,
daisies, meadow buttercups, and crisp plain grass rooted in the soil
held flat by feet and hooves, then toothed and ground into a slimy
gist, into a spit that would produce the milk for Zhenya's yogurt.
How I held my mouth ready for that pink liquid, how in it I tasted
my own bare feet running after a butterfly across the pasture.
As if Zhenya went with us everyplace, memorizing us into her
disoriented inadequacy. As if we were two graceful puppets in the
hands of a clumsy puppeteer.

In spring we sat on the fire escape in the courtyard of the
opera house, your face so small that I could hardly see it behind
your cigarette, somebody rehearsing in a window above. We were
splitting up. I was relieved the split was out there on the table, and
you had to eat it, otherwise, as if not your mother then somebody
must have told you, you'd never grow up, never kill the dragon.
Your hands were shaking. To keep your mind off it, I asked you to
teach me smoking. And so you were teaching me, and I smoked,
and coughed, and burned, until I disappeared.

Opera

opera
is a fish market
where fish sing with the silver of their flesh
the conductor plunges the knife
and from the nets of the singers' lungs
deepwater fish fall out

when in agony on the cutting board
in a hysterical search for the seawater
fish lick the sweat from their monger's hands
and gulp the dripping-on-the-floor blood
hoping to stuff it back into their bodies –
silver scales melt into a bullet
and the bullet aims at the fish's gills –
sing!

how could a fish know under the water
that it took from the hook not the bait
but a note
that a pole made by Stradivari
would bite at its heart like a serpent
three times –
hosanna! hosanna! hosanna!
three chimes –
for father, spirit, and son.

who are you – a conductor or priest?
is it a baton or a cross?
sh-h-h-h

opera

not earrings your Carmen wears but tambourines
her heart like a horn lives off the lips
no blood in her veins but saliva of kisses
her blood she wears outside as a dress
oh Carmen! we smuggle into the night
the cargo you hid inside our ears

Don José! slim like a knife's blade
you will write the last note
on scores of the Gypsy's ribs

opera!
voice tasting on an empty stomach!
vineyards of your wardrobes!
i would run through them barefoot
with a wasp in my ear toward
your curtain parting like a great sea
your voices departing bodies like big ships
and voyaging until they hit silence

Jean-Paul Belmondo

It begins with your face of stone
where lips repose like two seals
in a coastal mist of cigarette smoke
you move through the streets –
listing them
is as useless as naming waves.

> (This city is so handsome for a reason –
> it was made out of your rib.)

It continues with my
skidmarked-by-a-dress
body.

> I stand on the border
> in heels like sixth toes
> and show you
> where to park.

> That very night
> lying together
> > in the dogs' yard
> – flowers are biting my back! –
> you whisper:
> > the longer I look on the coins of your nipples
> > the clearer I see the Queen's profile.

For you, body and money are the same
as the chicken and the egg.
The metaphor of "a woman's purse"

> escapes you.

Stealing, you like to mumble:

a purse is a purse is a purse is a purse.

Also:

a real purse in your hand is worth

two metaphorical purses over your mouth.

They tell me

you are a body

anchored to the shore by its rusting blood.

Your wound darkens on your chest like a crow.

I tell them

                — as agreed — that you are my youth.

An apple that bit into me to forget its own knowledge.

Death hands you every new day like a golden coin.

As the bribe grows

it gets harder to turn it down.

Your heart of gold gets heavier to carry.

Your hands know that a car has a waist

and a gun — a lobe.

You take me where the river once lifted its skirts

and God, abashed with that view,

ordered to cover that shame with a city.

That city's dance square

shrunk by the darkness to the size

of a sleeping infant's slightly open mouth.

I cannot tell between beggars' stretched hands

                and dogs' dripping tongues.

You cannot tell between legs –

      mine –

           tables' –

               chairs' –

                    others'.

That dance square is a cage
where accordions grin at dismembered violin torsos.
Beggars lick thin air off their lips.
Women whirling in salsa slash you
across the chest with the blades
of their skirts soiled in peonies.

Island

Rash of the harbor lights in the mountain region.
Night, he says, is the dark humor of the day —
first you are scared
                    but by the sunrise
                              I'll get you laughing.
My head, thrown back in laughter, has bought me more
than money thrown forward, and men
pressed me down and worked like a Chinese seamstress.
But none could slap my face as hard as the sea slaps
its adopted child and steps back, all tears.

This island spat out by the sun over the world's shoulder,
a fence holds the bougainvillea laughter behind its teeth,
a metal gate guards the doze of heat-stricken watchdogs.
A road comes up to my face and stands like a mirror
showing everything that has led me to it: a bed
soft like bruised fruit, a whole lime garden bruised
by the afternoon shade, and his book's hard spine
breaking with the day.

A body strips down all the way to forgiveness
and grants itself before there's even a reason, unless
it wants to tell the other: I forgive
your juices for not filling these hard fruit;
your skin for not cracking and rotting over the ants'
heads; I forgive your throat for not birthing the dog's cough;
I forgive your hand, right now rising, falling, and leaving trace

unlike what it praises; I forgive your shadow for never becoming
a stain to mark this road, this bed, but mostly this sea.

Bricks of gray moonlight fall weightlessly
through the wooden
                              shades
building a new wall above the sink.
Here he lies on his stomach –
the gap between his ass and his thighs
forms a perfect black diamond.

Horizon blistered by the setting sun heals, leaving
a hardly visible scar.

About the Author

Valzhyna Mort was born in Minsk, Belarus, and moved to the United States in 2005. She made her American debut with the poetry collection *Factory of Tears* (Copper Canyon Press, 2008). In Slovenia she has received the Crystal of Vilenica poetry award, and in Germany the Hubert Burda Prize for Eastern European authors. In 2010 she was awarded the Lannan Foundation Fellowship and the Bess Hokin Prize from the Poetry Foundation.

ACKNOWLEDGMENTS

I would like to thank the editors of the following publications, in which these poems first appeared: *Guernica, Gulf Coast, Narrative, Poetry, Poetry International, The Portland Review, Southword, Town, Tuesday; An Art Project, Wolf Magazine.*

"Crossword" was reprinted in *So Much Things to Say: Over 100 Poets from the First Ten Years of the Calabash International Literary Festival,* edited by Kwame Dawes and Colin Channer.

A selection of poems from this book was reprinted in *American Odysseys: Writings by New Americans,* the Vilcek Foundation's anthology of prominent young immigrant writers.

I am deeply thankful to the following people and institutions: Lannan Foundation; Sylt Quelle and Internationales Haus der Autoren Graz, the two artist residences where most of this book was written, and there, respectively, Indra Wussow and Luise Grinschgl; Alice Yard; my editor Michael Wiegers and everyone at Copper Canyon Press.

Since 1972, Copper Canyon Press has fostered the work of emerging, established, and world-renowned poets for an expanding audience. The Press thrives with the generous patronage of readers, writers, booksellers, librarians, teachers, students, and funders — everyone who shares the belief that poetry is vital to language and living.

Copper Canyon Press gratefully acknowledges board member

JIM WICKWIRE

for his many years of service to poetry and independent publishing.

MAJOR SUPPORT HAS BEEN PROVIDED BY:

THE **PAUL G. ALLEN**
FAMILY *foundation*

Lannan

NATIONAL
ENDOWMENT
FOR THE ARTS

WASHINGTON STATE
ARTS COMMISSION

The Paul G. Allen Family Foundation

Amazon.com

Anonymous

Diana and Jay Broze

Beroz Ferrell & The Point, LLC

Golden Lasso, LLC

Gull Industries, Inc.
on behalf of William and Ruth True

Lannan Foundation

Rhoady and Jeanne Marie Lee

National Endowment for the Arts

Cynthia Lovelace Sears and Frank Buxton

Washington State Arts Commission

Charles and Barbara Wright

To learn more about underwriting
Copper Canyon Press titles, please call
360-385-4925 X103

Lannan Literary Selections

For two decades Lannan Foundation has supported the
publication and distribution of exceptional literary works.
Copper Canyon Press gratefully acknowledges their support.

LANNAN LITERARY SELECTIONS 2011

Michael Dickman, *Flies*

Laura Kasischke, *Space, in Chains*

Deborah Landau, *The Last Usable Hour*

Valzhyna Mort, *Collected Body*

Dean Young, *Fall Higher*

RECENT LANNAN LITERARY SELECTIONS
FROM COPPER CANYON PRESS

Stephen Dobyns, *Winter's Journey*

David Huerta, *Before Saying Any of the Great Words: Selected Poems*,
translated by Mark Schafer

Sarah Lindsay, *Twigs and Knucklebones*

Heather McHugh, *Upgraded to Serious*

W.S. Merwin, *Migration: New & Selected Poems*

Taha Muhammad Ali, *So What: New & Selected Poems, 1971–2005*,
translated by Peter Cole, Yahya Hijazi, and Gabriel Levin

Travis Nichols, *See Me Improving*

Lucia Perillo, *Inseminating the Elephant*

James Richardson, *By the Numbers*

Ruth Stone, *In the Next Galaxy*

John Taggart, *Is Music: Selected Poems*

Jean Valentine, *Break the Glass*

C.D. Wright, *One Big Self: An Investigation*

For a complete list of Lannan Literary Selections from
Copper Canyon Press, please visit Partners on our Web site:
www.coppercanyonpress.org

The poems are set in Perpetua, a typeface that was designed by English sculptor, typeface designer, stonecutter, and printmaker Eric Gill. Book design and composition by Phil Kovacevich. Printed on archival-quality paper at McNaughton & Gunn, Inc.

The Chinese character for poetry is made up of two parts: "word" and "temple." It also serves as pressmark for Copper Canyon Press.